TLC for Teenagers & their Parents

To Emily:

TLC creates a beautiful Ballet dancer, and great teenager:

Kind turnout;

Yvonne Kamerling

TLC for Teenagers & their Parents

Inspirational Quotes, Poetry, Touching Stories

Yvonne Kamerling

iUniverse, Inc.
New York Lincoln Shanghai

For my daughter

Yvette Rose

You are the light of my life.

Thank you for just being you.

Mummy (Mom)

Tender Loving Care

Creates universal happiness.

It illuminates your life's journey.

Contributors

Rob Elder, whose poetry appears in this book, lives in Brunswick, Maine, and has two teenagers. His poetry has appeared in the Colby College Poetry Review, and been read at various events in New England. He is the author of the poetry book *Sky Road*.

John Keatts and Heather Ganz have contributed short stories.

Contents

➢ INTRODUCTION xix

➢ DEFINING TLC 1
  • THE KINDNESS 1
  • TENDER LOVING CARE 3
  • WHAT IS TENDER LOVING CARE, OR TLC? 5
  • WEAR YOUR BRAND OF TLC 7
  • WHAT'S IN IT FOR ME? 9
  • A TENDER PRESENCE AND WARMTH 11
  • THE HEART THAT IS OPEN 13
  • JOYS SHARED WITH ALL THEIR FRIENDS 15
  • HER LAST MOMENTS… 16

➢ TLC COOKBOOK 21
  • NOTES FROM THE TLC COOKBOOK… 21
  • RECIPES FOR SUCCESSFUL TLC 21
  • 'TIME ZONE' PIE 23
  • MAGNIFICENT MILKSHAKE 25

➢ HAPPINESS 27
  • WHAT IS HAPPINESS? 27
  • IT IS OFTEN SAID THAT 29
  • WHERE IS HAPPINESS? 31
  • MISS ROSE 32

➤ YOU AND YOUR PARENTS 39
  • WHY DO YOUR PARENTS NEED YOUR TLC? 39
  • TLC MAKES YOUR PARENTS FEEL SPECIAL 41
  • HOW SPECIAL IS SPECIAL? 43
  • SEPTEMBER 11, 2001 44
  • LEFT ALONE 49
  • WHAT DO YOUR PARENTS MEAN TO YOU? 51
  • DID YOUR PARENTS TAKE TLC 101? 53
  • HOW CAN YOU GIVE TLC TO YOUR PARENTS? ..55
  • LOCKS OF LOVE 56
  • TLC FOR TOXIC PARENTS 61
  • MILLIONS OF PURE DROPS 63

➤ RECOGNIZING TLC 65
  • RECONIZING THE NEED OF OTHERS IS
    THE GREATEST GIFT 65
  • ACCEPTING PAIN, ANGER,
    SADNESS AND GRIEF 67
  • WHAT ARE THE LONG-TERM EFFECTS
    OF TLC? 69
  • HELPING HANDS 70
  • CALM ABIDING 73

➤ TOTAL LIFE COACHING 75
  • WHY NOT COACH YOUR PARENTS? 75
  • TRY TOTAL LIFE COACHING 77
  • HEARTS ON FIRE 79
  • WHY ME? 81
  • WISH LIST 82
  • COACHING QUESTIONS THAT FEEL GOOD... 85
  • ALONE IS GONE 87

➢ TOTAL TLC 88
  • GOLDEN YEARS 88
  • COMBINE THE TWO TLC'S AND
    WHAT DO YOU GET? 91
  • ALWAYS THERE 93

➢ MY NOTES 95
  • TLC NOTES FOR ME 96
  • TLC NOTES FOR MY FRIENDS 97
  • TLC NOTES FOR MY PARENTS 98
  • TLC NOTES FOR MY GRANDPARENTS 99
  • TLC NOTES FOR THE WORLD 100

List of Illustrations

1. The Kindness 1
2. Tender Loving Care 2
3. What Is Tender Loving Care, Or TLC? 4
4. Wear Your Brand Of TLC 6
5. What's In It For Me? 8
6. A Tender Presence 10
7. The Heart 12
8. Joys Shared 14
9. Her Last Moments 18
10. Notes From The TLC Cookbook 20
11. 'Time Zone' Pie 22
12. Magnificent Milkshake 24
13. What Is Happiness? 26
14. It Is Often Said 28
15. Where Is Happiness? 30
16. Why Do Your Parents…? 38
17. Tender Loving Care Makes Parents… 40
18. How Special Is Special? 42
19. Left Alone 48
20. What Do Your Parents Mean To You? 50
21. Did Your Parents Take TLC 101? 52
22. How Can You Give TLC To Your Parents? 54
23. TLC For Toxic Parents 60
24. Millions Of Pure Drops 62
25. Recognizing The Need Of Others… 64

26. Accepting Pain… 66

27. What Are The Long-Term Effects…? 68

28. Calm Abiding 72

29. Why Not Coach Your Parents? 74

30. Try Total Life Coaching 76

31. Hearts On Fire 78

32. Why Me? 80

33. Coaching Questions That Feel Good 84

34. Alone Is Gone 86

35. Combine The Two TLCs… 90

36. Always There 92

37. TLC Notes For Me 96

38. TLC Notes For My Friends 97

39. TLC Notes For My Parents 98

40. TLC Notes For My Grandparents 99

41. TLC Notes For The World 100

Acknowledgements

My heartfelt gratitude to those friends whose creative ideas and amazing energy helped make this book a reality, and to my family for believing in me.

Many thanks to **Rob Elder** for his wisdom and beautiful poetry.

Rosetta Stone for all her hard efforts in designing brilliant illustrations.

Thank you **Janet Yudewitz,** for graciously giving of your time and effort…

I also acknowledge and thank **John Keatts** for his stories, generosity, and support.

Thanks to **Maggie Wright** for assisting me with a change of direction…

To **Phil Whitmarsh** of iUniverse for his help and encouragement…

And **Heather Ganz** for sharing her stories and loving the idea of a book about TLC.

Introduction

Teenagers often look outward for answers to their happiness by emulating sport, rock, and movie stars. How wonderful would their world be if they found an inner glamour that would light up and bring joy into their lives? TLC is not known as a hero. It does not appear on TV, in a video or at a concert. It is not hounded by the paparazzi or worn on designer clothes. TLC is found in our hearts. *This book conveys a continuous message and is a keep-sake that will open up teenagers' hearts...and the hearts of their parents. It allows them to pursue and discover their own answers and to feel a sense of who they really are, and who they want to be.*

I always wanted to be a person who could put compassion and TLC back into those empty pockets, passing my generosity and kindness to all. As a mother, a teacher, a life coach, a motivational speaker, and, now, an author, sending love to others has always been natural for me. I always knew that I had an abundance of love to give. TLC is a gift. It is needed in everything we do. I have personally found TLC to be the biggest part of my continuing life journey. It has been, is, and always will be the motivating force in my life.

Throughout my years as a teacher, I always wanted to help my students find the lighter side of life and experience an easier path to happiness. I felt I could not touch all their hearts, but now I have the chance to do so. This book enables me to guide the lives of teenagers and their parents, and give them a deeper sense of wisdom.

Life coaching brings an awareness and sense of purpose into the lives of my clients. Combining Total Life Coaching and TLC creates a conscious path toward self-fulfillment and happiness.

Happiness is not fabricated; it comes as a deep and insightful part of our intrinsic selves. Finding enough love and compassion to help others be happy is a universal calling and a creative measure that will ensure successful TLC.

The Kindness

Of naturally helping others

To dance

In the *see* of life

Is the greatest gift

We can give each other.

We call this:

Tender

Loving

Care

What Is Tender Loving Care, Or TLC?

It is an emotion that is eternal.

It is a way of being close to others.

It is feeling what others feel.

It is a process of connecting.

It is the energy flow that binds us.

It helps us feel, eat, and sleep better.

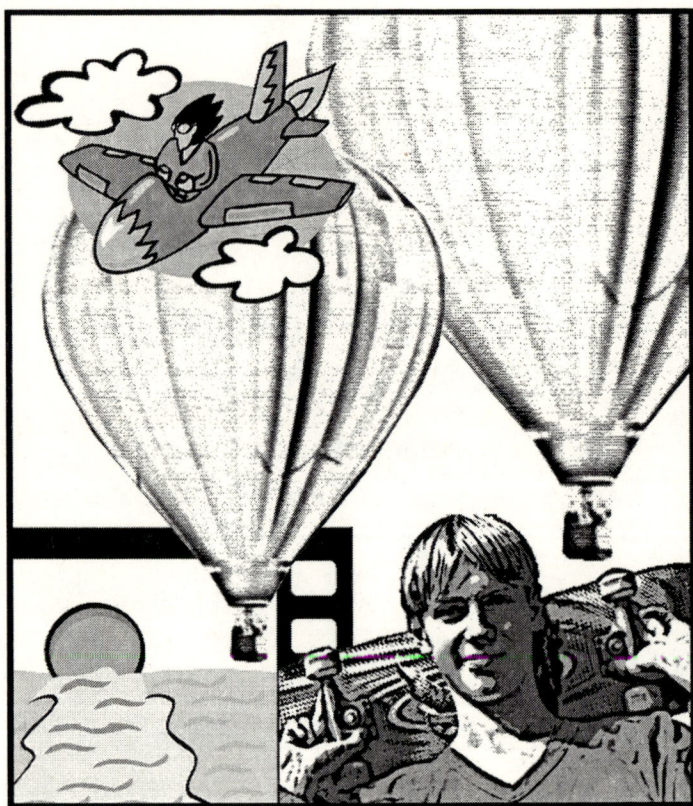

Wear Your Brand of TLC

Helping other humans creates vibes.

It brings us back to the center of gravity.

It is like going through airline turbulence:

a little light chop, then coming out of

the bumpiness into calmness.

It helps us to improve our perspective on life.

It helps us to link up with our parents and friends.

It gives us that special image that makes

others around us feel good.

What's in It for Me?

TLC is kool!!! It is hip. It is in style.

What do you get back?

Well, nothing that you can decorate your room with;

nothing that you can wear; nothing that you can eat.

Those are outward attachments.

TLC is an inner costume that makes you feel good.

It makes you grow to love everything around you.

It makes you appreciate your parents,

your revolving world.

A tender presence and warmth

Fill the heart with a loving

So sweet like drops of morning dew.

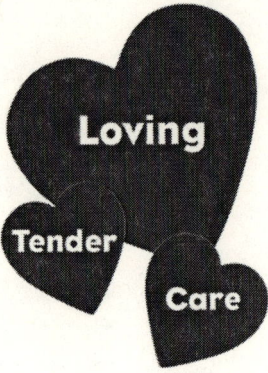

Loving

Tender

Care

Write   Write   Write

My Thoughts

The heart that is open

Too often

Finds friends

Where others simply

Find passersby along the road.

Joys shared with all their friends

Emerge as love

And points to the constant

Yearning

For the recognition of connection

Awake in us all.

Her Last Moments...

I had my heart set on a black kitten
and scouted the animal shelter from top to bottom,
but there were no black cats.
But then I saw, tucked away next to a humongous
old gray cat, a small black kitten with a
white star on her chest.
I named her Inky.

Inky came to our house a timid cat.
She used to hide underneath
the refrigerator and couch,
but over time, she became my soul mate,
my best friend, my sweet bundle of fur.

Her favorite activity was to curl up in my lap and purr.
She also loved to play with a tiny ball with a bell in the
middle; we had so much fun. I protected her from harm,
and she protected me from loneliness...

Inky lived for 22 years, quite an achievement for a cat.
She spent the last day of her life
saying good-bye to my family and friends.
During her last night, we spent hours
cuddled up together. She grew weaker and weaker.
As her final time approached, she looked at me and
meowed three times. Then she lifted her head into the
crook of my arms.

Her breath was shallow and short.
As she lay in my arms, we connected.
There was silence.

Her spirit and my soul opened up to each other.
So much trusting love passed between us.
We were united in life and death.

Her death enabled me to reach out compassionately to
all creatures in this world.

Now I connect differently with animals,
knowing they have an equal place on this earth.
Their lives are just as important as mine.
Thank you, my dear feline companion!

Notes from the TLC Cookbook...

Recipes for Successful TLC

Being in charge of your

daily 604,800 thoughts

can generate compassion and tenderness.

It creates Loving Care,

which is a fabulous part of human nature.

'Time Zone' Pie

Knowing that you are an integral part of

our global community helps you to recognize

that you are in a continuous "change time zone."

Eliminating the unessential can create awesome ideas.

Magnificent Milkshake

Acknowledging your inner strength

and permanent light energy

can make you feel so complete.

It fills you with kindness, compassion,

and ultimate happiness.

What is Happiness?

It is a wonderful, rich emotion filled with laughter and

joyful feelings of elation and peace of mind.

It helps you become aware of the kindness of mankind

and

not their faults.

Others enjoy happiness through your TLC.

What a great way to improve

your perspective on life.

It is often said that

Friends are few, companions many;

But kindness to all

Brings the flowers of friendship

To many trees and gardens

Along our way.

Where is Happiness?

We all want it. How do we find it?

Look for it down the amber and red highway of love,

driving ahead, spreading TLC, creating happiness.

This real road connects you to your family and friends.

It sparks a glow of warmth throughout.

Miss Rose

Ryan was at it again…no homework…
fooling around in class.
Miss Rose was his fifth-grade teacher.
She wondered why he was always absent.
How could she stop his
self-destructive behavior?

Miss Rose spoke with his fourth-grade teacher, Miss Miller
and then with his third-grade teacher, Miss Powell.
Ryan had started his fourth-grade class well.
But, in the second half, he was about to fail.
Miss Miller had tried to coach him on his failing subjects,
but to no avail.

*His third-grade teacher
explained that Ryan's mother had become ill and
died during the holiday vacation.
His work and attendance had deteriorated
from that point on.*

*Ryan's teacher said that
Ryan had been a pleasure to have in class,
a natural-born leader.*

*Miss Rose now looked at Ryan with different eyes.
She could sense what he was feeling and
what he had lost.*

She wanted to make a difference in his life.
So she kept him after school
and asked him about his family.
Ryan explained what she already knew.

Then Miss Rose asked a very important question.
"What would your mother
think about you now?"
Ryan was silent.

As the year progressed,
Ryan's behavior in class improved.
He raised his hand during class frequently.
His childhood years passed quickly. He left Miss Rose's class
and continued to do well through grade school.

Years later, Miss Rose received an invitation from Ryan to
his high-school graduation. He was the valedictorian.
At the reception, Ryan hugged her and told her she was his
favorite teacher.

Four years later, another invitation arrived.
It was for Ryan's college graduation.
He said he had received help from many,
but that Miss Rose was still his favorite teacher.
When he graduated from medical school,
she was there.
She was still his favorite teacher.

Several years later, there was a message from
Dr. Ryan Crew.
He invited her to lunch.

During lunch he informed her that he was a medical
practitioner, that he had married and had a daughter
named Rose.
He grabbed Miss Rose's hand and said,
"You've made all of this possible.
You are still my favorite teacher."
Miss Rose replied, "No, Ryan.
You were my favorite teacher.
I was your student. Before you were in my class,
I taught math and English.
But you taught me how to teach people."

Why Do Your Parents Need Your TLC?

Because they don't understand who you are

and what became of you.

It can change your relationship

with the very people who claim to manage your

world.

You can grow to know them.

TLC bridges the generation gap.

Tender Loving Care Makes Your Parents Feel Special

It shows them that you care enough to make it happen.

TLC helps bind you to the representatives of your

birthday.

It can inspire them when guiding you through all the

stages of perpetual growth.

How Special Is Special?

It helps produce a new level of love and mutual respect.

It can make you feel in-touch.

It can reduce and eliminate conflicts.

What bliss to be best friends with your parents!

In your moment—their moment too—

is an enjoyable experience.

SEPTEMBER 11, 2001

A rescue worker on a boat that ferried
New Yorkers to New Jersey related this to me.
Shortly after the collapse of the second tower in lower
Manhattan, a middle-aged man covered in white dust,
wearing a business suit and carrying a briefcase,
came aboard the boat.

He was staggering and seemed troubled,
hardly able to propel himself to a seat.
The rescue worker asked if he could help.
There was no response.

He escorted the man to a seat and removed
his sunglasses. All that stared back were the
whites of the man's eyes.

At that moment, a young man about 18-years-old,
who was wearing a tank top and sneakers
and had long black dredlocks,
turned to the worker and said,
"You have enough to do.
Let me take over and help this man."

He put his arm around the man.
The shell-shocked man put his head on the teen's shoulder.
The rescue worker was grateful, as there were so many
people who needed attention.

The boat arrived on the New Jersey shore, and the
rescue worker who was helping people off the boat saw the
young man again.

He was helping the businessman toward the exit of the boat
and reiterated that he would
take care of the man.

On September 10, 2001,
the dark young man and the
businessman would have passed each
other on the streets of New York
without a word of greeting.

Left alone

The heart naturally

Finds friends in the

Kindness

Of a thousand faces

Awake in us all.

What Do Your Parents Mean to You?

They are the secure comfort behind your teenage fears,

a motivational force to adulthood.

It is their strength that helps you stay centered under

all conditions and circumstances.

You accept that raising you was a unique

learning process for them.

They are your caretakers.

Did Your Parents Take TLC 101?

No, you taught them how to be parents....

Way to go!

What you did was to change your outlook and position,

and so did they.

TLC helps you to blend,

accepting each other for what you are

and who you are.

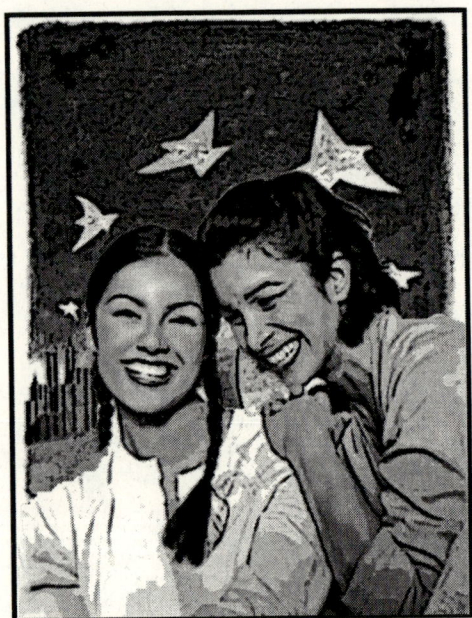

How Can You Give TLC to Your Parents?

You can open up your teenage heart

and let them in.

Precious connections....

TLC can bring you together in a most remarkable way.

It helps you share your memories and

life's experiences.

Locks of Love

Michele had the most beautiful hair.
It was blond with red highlights.
There was a slight wave to it.
It had a silken glow that created a halo around her head.
Wherever she went, people commented on how lucky she
was that her hair was naturally lovely.
She should become a model or
a movie star.

One of Michele's favorite television shows was
all about angels.
Well, actually, it was her mom's favorite show.
So Michele would share some time with her Mom on
Sunday nights, watching the show.
On one particular episode, the main character had lost her
hair because of cancer.

Michele wondered what it would be like to lose her hair,
her pride and joy.
What would it feel like to be sick and to lose one's hair?
How devastating.
What could she do to help?

The next day, Michele spoke to her guidance counselor
about the TV show and her feelings. The counselor sug-
gested that she check out an organization called
"Locks of Love."

A week later, Michele was sitting in a chair in the
kitchen of her home. Her mother had a
pair of scissors in her hand.

They were about to cut off seven inches of Michele's hair
and donate it to Locks of Love,
which makes wigs for children who have lost their hair.
The wigs are made from authentic hair and
children can even wear them when they are swimming.

Michele has grown and cut her hair twice so far. She is
determined to continue growing and donating her hair
until it grows gray. Watching her Sunday night show had
created a new angel!

TLC for Toxic Parents...

They need help.

It helps to understand that they are not evil.

They are confused and angry.

It is never your fault.

Keep liking and loving your true nature.

Pen   Pen   Pen

My Thoughts

Millions of pure drops

Falling softly

Filter our world.

Reconizing the Need of Others is the Greatest Gift

It is all about caring for mankind

in a real and genuine way,

sharing in the deepest of emotions.

It turns friendships into great friendships.

It puts so much positive direction into your life.

Accepting Pain, Anger, Sadness and Grief

Takes a portion of you that we call

TLC.

You can help,

So let go….

No holding back.

What are the Long-Term Effects of TLC?

You become one with your eternal self.

All is well in your world.

It makes you feel so healthy.

It creates plenty of energy.

Your skin glows.

You regain your appetite for life.

It helps balance your creative center.

HELPING HANDS

Heather looked at the classroom clock and made a mental note. As soon as the class was over, she would eat her energy bar (no time for lunch) and rush to the other end of the school. That is where the students with special needs were busily involved in an art project.

Heather had started a club that she called "Helping Hands." Her club sponsored students with mental retardation or autism, and those who were physically handicapped (perhaps confined to wheelchairs).

Heather had spent many lunch hours assisting the kids with this latest art project. The students and the Helping Hand members were making a quilt. It was a creation of love. When it was finished, it was going to be donated to "Project Linus," an organization for other children in need

As Heather hurried down the hallway, she gave thanks that she was one of the lucky teenagers that was healthy and able to walk that day.

Think   Think   Think

My Thoughts

Calm abiding

Insight and laughter

These all lead the heart

Into the confidence

Of knowing.

Why Not Coach Your Parents?

You can make a difference in your

parents' lives by coaching them.

TLC can help them achieve their goals

through Total Life Coaching.

You can make it possible for them to

connect with you.

Try Total Life Coaching

Coaching bridges the stand-still gap,

moving you into real action.

It prioritizes the complexities of your life.

It helps you focus on the

ideas at hand.

Hearts on fire

We connect in one big space

Light and formless

Moving on.

Why Me?

Listen to your own wisdom, that sacred knowledge

of your teenage heart.

When your parents speak,

listen very carefully.

It helps to make the pearl of happiness a brightly lit

connection between

you and them.

Could their visions be your visions?

Wish List

Everyone had written out their holiday wish list and passed
them around; so that they would get all the gifts they asked
for. Mom and Dad had looked at their
youngest daughter's list.
It had 20 items on it, from a new computer to three pairs of
designer jeans.
Then they checked out 18-year-old Lisa's list.
and they were surprised!

Lisa had asked for no presents.
Instead, she wanted all of the money that her parents
would have spent on gifts to go to needy families in the
community.
Her parents approached her with tenderness, which
included deep and grateful recognition of
Lisa's thoughtfulness and consideration.

Coaching Questions That Feel Good...

It is about asking permission, so that they can interpret

the essence of your present reality.

It helps to ask questions that are

important in your life.

How do you feel when I get a bad report card?

What's the problem when I drive

with my friends?

How much allowance is enough?

Hot   Hot   Hot

My Thoughts

Alone is gone

Into the healing heart

The sun of kindness

Burning effortlessly.

GOLDEN YEARS

Sara couldn't leave her job where she had
volunteered for so long. She loved to help the
elderly with all the fun activities that they did
on a daily basis. She organized bingo,
sing-alongs and sittercize (wheelchair activities).
Sara and her grandmother had been so close.
They had shared so many special times together,
not realizing how brief and precious
that time was.
Working with the elderly had made Sara feel closer to
the memories of her grandmother and to
accepting her mortality.

Her parents had told her to get a real job,
one that paid money. But how could she leave all of those
grandmas and grandpas whom she loved so much?
One day as she was hugging an elderly woman, and
listening to her explain that Sara's hugs always
made her day,
a supervisor noticed Sara's genuine feelings of exuberance,
compassion, and love.
A week later, Sara was asked if she'd like to become a
permanent member of the staff, a job that paid real money
and would finance her college education.

Combine the Two TLC's and What Do You Get?

You receive a vision of completeness,

armfuls of fun and laughter.

It helps you love and be loved.

It can provide you with peace and harmony.

You connect to and belong to all other

human beings.

It is UNIVERSAL.

TLC   TLC   TLC

My Thoughts

Always there.

Always loving.

This floating world

Within our familiar forms

Ineffable, precise.

My Notes

TLC Notes For Me

TLC Notes For My Friends

TLC Notes For My Parents

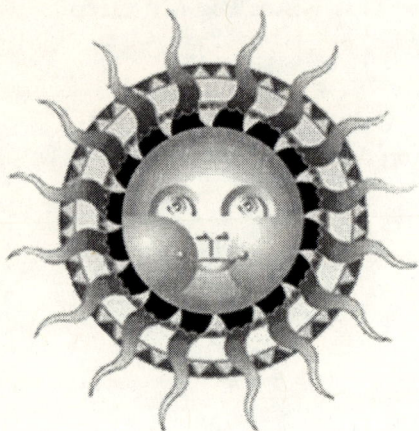

TLC Notes For My Grandparents

TLC Notes For The World

TLC for Teenagers & their Parents

Purchase this book from
your favorite bookstore, or online from iUniverse,
Amazon.com, BarnesAndNoble.com

www.yvonnekamerling.com

0-595-31583-6